COMMUNICATION STUDIES 103

Fundamentals of Speech Communication

Student Handbook

Kristine Greenwood
Marshall University

Kendall Hunt
publishing company

www.kendallhunt.com
Send all inquiries to:
4050 Westmark Drive
Dubuque, IA 52004-1840

ISBN 978-1-4652-2645-7

Printed in the United States of America

10 9 8 7 6

Contents

Preface

For many of you, public speaking is a new and somewhat frightening subject to study. Yes, you will have to give speeches in this class. Hopefully, at the end of the course you will be more confident getting up in front of people and presenting them with your thoughts. It is a skill highly sought after by employers and will help you become a better citizen.

This handbook is designed to help you succeed in this course. It will help you:

1. Identify principles of public speaking
2. Analyze your strengths and weaknesses as a speaker
3. Research and organize your ideas
4. Present clear, coherent, informative speeches
5. Develop cogent arguments in persuasive speeches
6. Critically evaluate messages, both in class and outside class

Please bring this handbook to each class session!

Kristine L. Greenwood, PhD
Basic Course Director

Course Data

This section contains your general course syllabus (your instructor will also give you a supplemental course syllabus), a sheet to keep track of assignment dates and grades received, a student information sheet you should fill out and give to your instructor, and an audience analysis questionnaire to fill out and return to your instructor.

COMMUNICATION STUDIES 103

Fundamentals of Speech Communication
General Syllabus

CMM 103 Section # ______________________________

Instructor ______________________________

Office # ______________ Phone # ______________

E-mail address ______________________________

Office Hours ______________________________

Textbook: David Zarefsky. *Public Speaking: Strategies for Success*, 7th ed., 2013.

Course Description: A course designed to enhance the development of critical-thinking skills and their application to verbal and nonverbal interaction in interpersonal and public communication contexts.

Course Philosophy: CMM 103 is a part of the university's general education requirements. We believe that communication is a fundamental and essential part of life. We also believe that improving both your understanding of communication and your ability to communicate effectively will serve you well in your career, your relationships, and your civic life. This course is designed to help you become more confident, more articulate, and better able to interpret the communication of others.

University Policies: By enrolling in this course, you agree to the University Policies listed below. Please read the full text of each policy at www.marshall.edu/academic-affairs/policiesStudents with Disabilities | Affirmative Action | Computing Services Acceptable Use Excused Absence (undergraduate) | Academic Dishonesty | Inclement Weather | MU Alert

Program Student Learning Outcomes

1. Specialized Knowledge
2. Broad Integrative Knowledge
3. Intellectual Skills: Analytic Inquiry
4. Intellectual Skills: Use of information resources
5. Intellectual Skills: Engaging diverse perspectives
6. Intellectual Skills: Quantitative fluency
7. Intellectual Skills: Communication fluency
8. Applied Learning
9. Civic Learning
10. Relationships among Course, Program, and Degree Profile Outcomes

Course Outcomes	How Accomplished in this Course	How Evaluated in this Course	Program Outcomes	Degree Profile Outcomes

Students will be able to recognize communication as a transactional process by

Course Outcomes	How Accomplished in this Course	How Evaluated in this Course	Program Outcomes	Degree Profile Outcomes
Determining audience orientation toward the topic .	Lecture Classroom activities Audience Evaluation Survey Peer Evaluations	Speech Proposals Oral Presentations Critical Listening Exam	1, 5, 7. 8	• 1, 5, 7. 8
Identifying supporting material most relevant to the audience	Lecture Activities Peer Evaluations	Speech Proposals Supporting a Claim Creating an Argument Oral Presentations Preparation Outlines Critical Listening Exam	1, 3, 4, 5, 7, 8	• 1, 3, 4, 5, 7, 8
Recognizing and adjusting to nonverbal audience feedback	Lecture Activities Peer Evaluations	Oral Presentations Critical Listening Exams	1 ,7, 8	• 1 ,7, 8

Students will learn to demonstrate critical thinking in the production and evaluation of communication events by

Course Outcomes	How Accomplished in this Course	How Evaluated in this Course	Program Outcomes	Degree Profile Outcomes
Differentiating between various types of evidence	Lecture Classroom Activities	Speech Proposals Supporting a Claim Creating an Argument Oral Presentations Preparation Outlines Exam	**1, 2, 3, 5, 7, 8, 9**	• **1, 2, 3, 5, 7, 8, 9**
Extrapolating valid claims from evidence	Lecture Classroom Activities	Creating an Argument Persuasive Speech Preparation Outlines Self Evaluation Critical Listening Exam	**1, 2, 3, 5, 7, 8, 9**	• **1, 2, 3, 5, 7, 8, 9**
Identifying and producing factual, value, and policy claims	Lecture Classroom Activities	Creating an Argument Speech Proposals Persuasive Speech Preparation Outlines Critical Listening Exam	**1, 2, 3, 5, 7, 8, 9**	• **1, 2, 3, 5, 7, 8, 9**
Identifying the types of reasoning that link evidence to claims	Lecture Classroom Activities	Creating an Argument Persuasive Speech Preparation Outlines Critical Listening Self Evaluation Exam	**1, 2, 3, 5, 7, 8, 9**	**1, 2, 3, 5, 7, 8, 9**
Identifying the limitations of evidence	Lecture Classroom Activities	Creating an Argument Persuasive Speech Critical Listening Exam	**1, 2, 3, 5, 7, 8, 9**	**1, 2, 3, 5, 7, 8, 9**

Identifying weaknesses in argument and reasoning	Lecture Classroom Activities Peer Evaluations	Creating an Argument Speech Proposals Persuasive Speech Critical Listening Self Evaluation Exam	**1, 2, 3, 5, 7, 8, 9**	**1, 2, 3, 5, 7, 8, 9**
Producing valid arguments	Lecture Classroom Activities Peer Evaluations	Creating an Argument Persuasive Speech Critical Listening Self Evaluation Exam	**1, 2, 3, 5, 7, 8, 9**	**1, 2, 3, 5, 7, 8, 9**

Students will produce organized informative and persuasive presentations by

Demonstrating the ability to capture audience attention,	Lecture Classroom Activities Peer Evaluations	Oral Presentations Preparation Outlines Speech Proposals Self Evaluation Critical Listening Exam	**1, 7**	**1, 7**
Stating the thesis and pre-viewing their oral remarks,	Lecture Classroom Activities Peer Evaluations	Oral Presentations Preparation Outlines Self Evaluation Critical Listening Exam	**1, 7**	**1, 7**
Using transitions and sign-posts to emphasize speech structure, and	Lecture Classroom Activities Peer Evaluations	Oral Presentations Preparation Outlines Self Evaluation Critical Listening Exam	**1, 7**	**1, 7**
Concluding their remarks with a summary of the main points	Lecture Classroom Activities Peer Evaluations	Oral Presentations Preparation Outlines Self Evaluation Critical Listening Exam	**1, 7**	**1, 7**

Students will develop effective extemporaneous speaking skills by

Maintaining eye contact with the audience while speaking	Lecture Classroom Activities Peer Evaluations	Oral Presentation Self Evaluation Critical Listening Exam	**1, 7**	**1, 7**
Using gestures which comple-ment the verbal message	Lecture Classroom Activities Peer Evaluations	Oral Presentation Self Evaluation Critical Listening Exam	**1, 7**	**1, 7**
Speaking with varied vocal cues	Lecture Classroom Activities Peer Evaluations	Oral Presentation Self Evaluation Critical Listening Exam	**1, 7**	**1, 7**

Attendance Policy: Regular attendance in this class is essential if you expect to succeed. In addition, attendance during speech presentations is mandatory. To pass this class you must perform all the oral speaking assignments on the date assigned, and you are expected to provide your fellow classmates with appropriate feedback. Each instructor will deduct points for your failure to participate as an audience member while others are presenting their speeches. Of course, university excused absences will be honored, and arrangements will made for makeup work. Absences not excused by the university and subsequent makeup work are subject to the discretion of your instructor. If possible, you should talk with your instructor prior to absences, but when not possible, you need to speak with your instructor as soon as possible after the absence to arrange for makeups.

Plagiarism Policy: All written and oral assignments should be your own work. Any supporting material (information and ideas) from other sources should be acknowledged in some way. Both oral and written footnotes are required for this course. Submitting work that is not original is considered academic dishonesty and taken seriously by the University, the College of Liberal Arts and the Department of Communication Studies. Penalties for academic dishonesty can range from a zero for the assignment to expulsion from the University. Academic dishonesty includes using speeches and outlines from other students or other sources and submitting or performing them as your own.

Video Recording Policy: With your permission, the basic public speaking program will use a random sample of the recorded persuasive speeches for an assessment of the program at the end of each semester. This assessment will help us evaluate and improve the class. Please sign, date and return the permission page found at the end of this handbook to your instructor.

Requirements:

Written assignments		
Informative speech proposal	40 points	
Persuasive speech proposal	40	
Supporting a claim	25	
Creating an argument	25	
Informative preparation outline	50	
Informative self-evaluation	15	
Persuasive speech preparation outline	50	
Persuasive self-evaluation	15	
Listening	30	
	Total points	290
Oral assignments (Speeches must be presented to an audience to pass the course)		
Introduction speech	20	
Informative speech	75	
Persuasive speech	100	
Ceremonial speech	50	
Impromptu speech	20	
	Total points	265
Exams		
Unit exams	120	
Final exam	100	
	Total points	220
TOTAL POINTS AVAILABLE		775

Grading:

A =	100–90%	775–697
B =	89–80%	696–620
C =	79–70%	619–542
D =	69–60%	541–465

Assignment Schedule and Tally Sheet

Assignments	Due Date	Points Earned
Introduction speech	______	______
Informative speech proposal	______	______
Supporting a claim	______	______
Informative speech & outline	______	______ ______
Informative self-evaluation	______	______
Persuasive speech proposal	______	______
Creating an argument	______	______
Persuasive speech & outline	______	______ ______
Persuasive self-evaluation	______	______
Ceremonial speech	______	______
Impromptu speech	______	______
Listening assignment	______	______

Exams	Date	Points Earned
Unit One	______	______
Unit Two	______	______
Final Exam	______	______
Quizzes & Extra Credit		______
Total Points Earned		______

Audience Analysis Sheet

Name: ______________________________ Student #: 901 ___________

Please fill out the following questionnaire and return to your instructor. This sheet will be used to assemble a general analysis of your audience according to the textbook chapter on audience analysis. You will be provided with a summary sheet so that you can adapt your speech topics and approach to your classmates. Feel free not to answer questions you are not comfortable with.

Audience Composition—Demographics

Age: ________ Sex: M F Family size: ______________

(Circle one) Single Married Widowed Urban Suburban Rural

Class standing: Fr So Jr Sr

Religious affiliation: ______________ Ethnic background: ______________

Reference groups: ______________________________

Audience Culture (interests and knowledge)

Favorite subjects in school:

Favorite music:

Favorite book:

Favorite activities (hobbies, sports, etc.):

Favorite movie or TV show:

The most important issues facing me are:

Socially:

Politically:

Locally:

Topics I am most interested in hearing or speaking about:

Audience Psychology (selective attention and exposure)

How often do you:

Read the local newspaper?

Watch the local news?

Read a national newspaper?

Watch national news?

Read news magazines?

Assignment Descriptions Sample Assignments

This section of the handbook contains descriptions of the course assignments. The rationale section tells you why the assignment is useful to you; the description section tells you what you are to do; and the considerations section tells you what will be taken into account by your instructor when grading the assignment. Also included are samples that you should follow when preparing your assignment for submission.

Speech of Introduction Assignment

Rationale

This speech is designed to provide you with a simple presentation that allows you to talk about something you know well and for you to get to know your fellow classmates. It is hoped you will become more comfortable speaking to an audience and with developing a speech.

Description

1. Prepare a **two- to three-minute** speech that reveals something about your personality, values, or beliefs.
2. Deliver the speech extemporaneously (using note cards).
3. Your speech should have an introduction, body, and conclusion. Use transitions between the main points.
4. Your speech should be organized in a way that makes it easy for your audience to follow, understand, and remember.
5. You should use supporting material that develops your main points.
6. Your speech should be delivered in an animated and enthusiastic manner while maintaining eye contact with your audience.
7. Your instructor will suggest some ways to approach your speech and the following suggestions may help you:
   a. Design a coat-of-arms that tells about your family origins.
   b. Bring in an object that represents your values, beliefs, or personality.
   c. Talk about someone you admire and would like to emulate.
   d. Tell how a favorite movie, book, poem, artwork, song, or TV show reflects your beliefs, values, or personality.

Considerations

1. Is the speech structure obvious and appropriate?
2. Does it have an introduction, body, and conclusion?
3. Did it gain the audience's attention?
4. Was the thesis clearly stated?
5. Did it preview the main points?
6. Was the body of the speech well supported?
7. Were the main points easily identified?
8. Were transitions or signposts used and obvious?
9. Did the conclusion include a summary and impact statement?
10. Did the speaker maintain eye contact throughout the speech?
11. Was the speaker vocally interesting?
12. Did the speaker use appropriate gestures?
13. Was the speech within the time requirements?

Sample Speech of Introduction

Name: ________________________________ Assignment: Speech of Introduction

Introduction

Attention Getter: Bring in a drawing of my coat of arms.

Thesis: Believe it or not but this drawing represents me.

Preview: These four flags tell you about my ancestry, my early years, my home, and my work.

Body

I. The upper left-hand corner is the flag of Norway.
   A. I am a first-generation American because my father was born in Norway.
   B. I can't speak the language because my father wouldn't teach me, but he did teach me a lot about the values and traditions of Norway.

Transition: However, Norway is far removed from my early years.

II. In the upper right-hand corner is the flag of New Jersey.
   A. I spent the first 22 years of my life in Bergen County, New Jersey.
   B. I hope you couldn't tell because as a speech major I've tried hard to lose my Jersey dialect and my Jersey attitudes.

Transition: But, Jersey is even further removed from my present home.

III. In the lower left-hand corner is the flag of West Virginia.
   A. I've spent more than half my life here in WV.
   B. I think I experienced more culture shock than my father did when he came to America.
   C. But I've come to admire the values of WV, and I'm glad I raised my children here.

Transition: For me WV values are embodied in my place of employment.

IV. In the lower right-hand corner is the Marshall University flag.
   A. Marshall is like a family with close ties to the community.
   B. Marshall is a strong place with strong traditions and values.

Conclusion

Summary: Like most adults I come from a great many places—Norway, New Jersey, West Virginia, Marshall University.

Final Appeal: All these places have had a great influence on me and who I am. I hope now you know me just a little better.

Critical Listening Assignment

Rationale

Accurate and critical listening is an important part of communication. This assignment is designed to help you put into practice and demonstrate the skills you learned in Chapter 4 of your textbook.

Description

1. Attend one of the many lectures and presentations given by guest speakers here on campus during the early part of the semester.
2. Write a three- to five-page paper describing the presentation using the mapping technique found in your textbook on pages 76–78 and describing your response to the presentation.
3. Your critical analysis should include complete descriptions of the following:
   Setting—Date and time of presentation. Description of the audience (size and make-up). Topic. General purpose.
   Speaker—Information about the speaker you gained prior to the presentation by the speaker. Qualifications for speaking about the topic. Impressions of speaker ethos.
   Introduction—Type and effectiveness of attention getter. Thesis sentence and clarity of the thesis. Audience disposition to topic and/or speaker. Preview of the main points.
   Body—Main points (complete sentences). Organizational pattern. Types of supporting material for each main point. Relevance and adequacy of supporting material to main points. Use of transitions.
   Conclusion—Adequacy of summary. Type and effectiveness of closing device.
   Delivery—Strongest and weakest aspects of delivery.
   Overall Impression of the Presentation—Did the speaker achieve his/her specific purpose? Was your knowledge expanded if an informative speech? Were the arguments compelling if a persuasive speech? What grade would you give the presentation?

Considerations

1. Was the presentation appropriate for this assignment?
2. Is the description of the presentation thorough? Was the mapping technique used correctly?
3. Was the overall impression justified by the description of the presentation? Does the completed assignment demonstrate critical listening?

Speech Proposal (Informative and/or Persuasive)

Rationale

This assignment is designed to help you select an appropriate topic for your speech and audience, begin gathering research, help you identify and select appropriate supporting materials, identify your general and specific purpose, develop a potential thesis statement, and identify an effective organizational structure for your speech. By completing this assignment and turning it in to your instructor on the due date, your instructor will have an opportunity to review your plans and provide constructive feedback.

Description

1. Identify your topic. The topic should be appropriate to the occasion (informative or persuasive), of interest to your audience, and of interest to you. See pages 120–127 in your textbook.
2. Provide a brief audience analysis for your speech by answering the following questions:
   What does your audience already know about your topic?
   What is their attitude toward your topic (positive or negative)?
   What beliefs or values do they hold about your topic?
   If an informative speech: What new information do they need?
   If a persuasive speech: What changes in beliefs, values, or behavior do they need and why?
3. Identify five (5) sources of information for your speech. *(Note: No more than two of your sources can be drawn from the Internet.)* The university library databases are a good source for your research. Be sure to use proper APA citations. See Chapter 7 in your textbook.
4. From the five sources you have identified, select eight items of supporting material. See pages 147–154 in your text for types of supporting material. You should include at least three different types of supporting material. Identify the type of supporting material you have selected and provide the appropriate footnote.
5. State your general purpose. See pages 128–132 in your text.
6. Draft your specific purpose statement: *I want my audience to . . .* See page 137 in the text.
7. Draft your thesis statement. See pages 137–140 in your textbook.
8. Identify an effective organizational pattern. See pages 219–224 in your text.

Considerations

1. Is the topic appropriate for the assignment?
2. Does the audience analysis help the speaker select sources, identify supporting material, and choose the appropriate general and specific purpose of the speech?
3. Are the sources credible? Are they properly cited?
4. Is the supporting material chosen with the audience and topic in mind? Are there a variety of types of supporting material? Are they properly identified as to type? Are they properly cited?
5. Is the general purpose consistent with either informative or persuasive speaking, depending on the assignment?
6. Does the specific purpose statement achieve the general purpose?
7. Does the thesis statement achieve the specific purpose statement? Is it a succinct statement of the central idea or claim of the speech?
8. Will the selected organizational pattern help the audience follow and remember the content of the speech?

Speech Proposal Assignment

Topic: Ronald Reagan

Sources:

Berger, M. (2004, June 6). Ronald Reagan dies at 93 [Electronic version]. *The New York Times.*

Marley, D. J. (2006). Ronald Reagan and the splintering of the Christian right. *Journal of Church and State, 48*(4), 851–868.

Medhurst, M. J. (1998). Writing speeches for Ronald Reagan: An interview with Tony Dolan. *Rhetoric & Public Affairs, 1*(2), 245–256.

Reagan, R. (1989, January 11). *Farewell address to the nation.* Retrieved June 16, 2010, from http://www.americanrhetoric.com/speeches/ronaldreaganfarewelladdress.html

Taylor, C. (2009). Role of a lifetime: Ronald Reagan and his revolution. *Dissent, 56*(3), 87–90.

Whitaker, R. W. (1998). Reagan, Ronald, and the media. *History of the Mass Media in the United States*, 576–578.

Supporting Material:

1. Testimony: In 1994, he touched the hearts of Americans when, in a handwritten letter, he let it be known he was suffering from [Alzheimer's disease]. "I now begin the journey that will lead me into the sunset of my life," Mr. Reagan wrote. "I know that for America there will always be a bright dawn ahead" (Berger, 2004, June 6).
2. Document: Ronald Wilson Reagan, a former film star who became America's 40th President, the oldest to enter the White House but imbued with a youthful optimism rooted in the traditional virtues of a bygone era, died yesterday [June 5, 2006] at his home in Los Angeles. He was 93 (Berger, 2004, June 6).
3. Statistic: "After Reagan's cuts in state aid, the town's center for the mentally retarded would close (1,200 jobs lost)" (Taylor, 2009, p. 87).
4. Opinion Testimony: "Ronald Reagan set out to make America into a place ruled by business, where those who fell by the wayside were merely succumbing to the inherent weakness that decreed they deserved to fail" (Taylor, 2009, p. 88).
5. Brief Example: "Reagan was kept isolated from reporters, often under the guise of security. Reporters complained of days passing with only distant glimpses of the President at ceremonial events, his staff maintaining a constant vigil to protect him from reporters' questions" (Whitaker, 1998, p. 577).
6. Anecdote: "America is respected again in the world and looked to for leadership. Something that happened to me a few years ago reflects some of this. It was back in 1981, and I was attending my first big economic summit, which was held that year in Canada" (Reagan, 1989).
7. Anecdote: "I was just going through the conservative political action committee speech (March 20, 1981) and I had forgotten how much of it he had written himself. It might have been a third, when you add up the ad-libs and the couple of lengthy inserts he put in" (Medhurst, 1998, p. 249).

8. Opinion Testimony: "The standard historiography of the era is that Reagan and George H. W. Bush supported the religious right's conservative social agenda, but they became too powerful, resulting in Clinton's victory in 1992. Recent history has shown that while many were writing the obituary of the Christian Right, it was actually growing in power" (Markley, 2006, p. 852).

Audience Analysis:

1. What does my audience know about this topic already?

My audience likely knows that Ronald Reagan served as President of the United States from 1981–1989. The audience is also probably aware that Ronald Reagan was a conservative Republican who served as President during the final years of the Cold War. Perhaps my audience also knows that Reagan was an actor before he entered a career in politics.

2. What positive and/or negative beliefs and values do they hold regarding this topic?

Depending on the political preferences of my audience, I would assume that they hold positive or negative beliefs and values about Ronald Reagan. Given the demographic makeup of my audience, I would assume that they hold positive beliefs and values about the topic.

3. What new information do they need and why?

Because this speech will focus on the life of Ronald Reagan, attention to his early life before he entered a career in politics will be necessary. Reagan's contribution to the history of the American presidency will also be explored.

General Purpose: Providing new information or perspective.

Specific Purpose: I want my audience to understand why Ronald Reagan was such a popular president.

Thesis Statement: Ronald Reagan connected in a unique way with the American electorate because of his life experiences.

Organizational Pattern: Chronological

Supporting a Main Point Assignment

Rationale

This assignment gives you the opportunity to practice developing a main point using supporting material that clarifies and expands the main point as well as practice in identifying the type of supporting material you will use. This is a written assignment, but your instructor may ask you to deliver the assignment as a speech.

Description

1. Write a simple declarative sentence that represents a main point in a speech. Use one of the main points that will be used in your informative speech.
2. State three items of supporting material that is directly related to that main point.
3. Identify the type of supporting material represented by each item.
4. Provide a complete citation using APA.

Considerations

1. Is the main point a simple, clear, and complete sentence?
2. Do the three selections of supporting material develop the main point as stated?
3. Are the three selections of supporting material identified correctly?
4. Are the three selections correctly cited?

Sample Supporting a Main Point Assignment

Name: ______________________________ Assignment: Supporting a Main Point

Main Point: We all need to become more critical consumers of persuasive messages.

Support 1. *Advertising Age* estimated that the average American sees, reads, or hears more than 5,000 persuasive advertising messages a day. (Statistic)

Larson, C. (2010). *Persuasion: Reception and Responsibility* (12th ed.). Wadsworth, p. 11.

Support 2. Television ad spots lead kids to perceive that every problem can be solved and that most can be solved by technology. (Opinion Testimony)

Postman, N. (1981). Interview. *U.S. News & World Report*, Jan. 19, p. 43.

Support 3. Recent research shows that persons who eat at Subway underestimate the calories in the meal and therefore, compensate with more snacks than Burger King lunch eaters, thus resulting in a higher caloric intake than if they had the Whopper to begin with. (Example)

Ithaca, J. S. (2007). *Time*, October 8, p. 65.

Preparation Outline Assignment

Rationale

All successful speeches begin with a preparation outline. This outline is a tool that you use to organize your ideas and research and it helps you check to make sure your speech is clearly understandable and easy to follow.

Description

1. You will include a report of your topic, general purpose, specific purpose, thesis, main points, and organizational pattern before you begin your outline. The thesis and main points should be cut and pasted from your outline.
2. You will label the outline introduction, body, and conclusion. See Chapter 10.
3. You will write out your introduction and conclusion in paragraph form and label the parts of each. See Chapter 10.
4. You will use the Roman numeral outline format for the body of the speech, clearly indicating coordination and subordination of ideas and supporting material. See Chapter 11.
5. All main points will be complete sentences. See Chapter 11.
6. Main points in the body of the speech will follow an obvious organizational pattern. See Chapter 9.
7. Transitions between main points will be labeled and written out as complete sentences. Please use the summary/preview format for transitions. See Chapter 10.
8. You will include in-text citations and a complete bibliography using APA style.
9. You will prepare a presentation outline based on the preparation outline using 3 X 5 note cards.

Considerations

1. Did the main points develop the thesis? Did the thesis achieve the specific purpose statement? Was the specific purpose statement consistent with the general purpose statement? Was the chosen organizational pattern appropriate for the topic and general purpose?
2. Does the outline use the Roman numeral format correctly?
3. Were the main points in complete sentences?
4. Were written-out transitions included?
5. Were supporting materials cited?
6. Were the main points organized in a recognizable manner?
7. Were the introduction and conclusion written out in paragraph form and were the parts of each labeled?
8. Were the sections of the outline (introduction, body, conclusion) clearly designated?
9. Was a complete bibliography using APA citations included?

Sample Preparation Outline

Name: ______________________ Assignment: Informative Speech

Topic:	Buddhism
General Purpose:	To provide new information or new perspective.
Specific Purpose:	I want my audience to understand some of the main ideas of Buddhism.
Thesis Statement:	Buddhism is based on the Four Nobel Truths that were taught by the Buddha and are ideas that can be applied to a person's life no matter what their religion may be.
Main Points:	The first three Noble Truths focus on the existence, the origin, and the cessation of creating. The fourth Noble Truth is the Noble Eightfold Path to end suffering.
Organizational Pattern:	Topical

Introduction

Attention Getter: The story of *The Thief and the Master.*

Influencing the Audience to View the Speaker Favorably: I was first introduced to Buddhism in a religious studies class. I had gone on a number of mission trips for my church but didn't feel I knew enough about other religions to speak convincingly. I thought that learning about other faiths would help me connect with others of different faiths.

Influencing the Audience to View the Topic Favorably: And I was right. If we try to understand other ideas without any bias because of the origins of those ideas, we often find that they are useful and valuable and can strengthen our own faith.

Thesis Statement: Buddhism is based on the Four Noble Truths that were taught by the Buddha and are ideas that can be applied to a person's life no matter what their religion.

Preview of the Main Points: Because I think these ideas may resonate with you or at least give you a clearer perspective of Buddhism, we will discuss the Four Noble Truths and the Eightfold Path to end suffering.

Body

I. The first three Noble Truths focus on the existence, the origin, and the cessation of creating.
   A. The first Nobel Truth is the existence of suffering.
      1. Thich Nhat Hanh states "we all suffer to some extent . . . We have to recognize and acknowledge the presence of this suffering and touch it" (Hanh 9).
      2. We have all experienced some sort of suffering and pain.
         a. The Bible focuses on using suffering to strengthen our faith and character.
         b. Buddhism also claims that one must truly feel and understand suffering before they may end it.
   B. The second Noble Truth is the origin of suffering.
      1. Thich Nhat Hanh says that the Buddha encouraged us to "recognize and identify the spiritual and material foods we have ingested that are causing us to suffer" (Hahn 11).
      2. We need to identify the beliefs or actions that have caused us to feel this way.
   C. The Third Noble Truth is the cessation of creating suffering.
      1. To do this we must refrain from doing those things that cause suffering for ourselves or for others.
      2. The Buddha taught that healing was possible.

Transition: Understanding suffering is important, but Buddhism teaches a way to end that suffering.

II. The fourth Noble Truth is the Noble Eightfold Path to end suffering.
   A. Right View involves a "deep understanding of the Four Noble Truths" and "having faith and confidence that there are people who have been able to transform their suffering" (Hanh 51).
   B. Right Thinking because thinking one thing and doing another destroys the unity of mind and body.
   C. Right Speech avoids causing others to suffer but instead encourages speaking of those things that bring joy and understanding.
   D. Right Action is dedication to nonviolence that Hanh describes as "touching love and preventing harm" (Hanh 60).
   E. Right Livelihood says that we should find work that does not force us to abandon love and compassion.
   F. Right Diligence is giving the proper attention and effort to everything we do.
   G. Right Mindfulness is crucial to maintaining all of the other practices.
      1. We should be aware at all times of what we think, say, and do.
      2. We hold dwell fully in the present and give attention and nourishment to those around us.
   H. Right Concentration includes both active and selective concentration.
      1. Active is focusing on what is happening in the present like when we are aware of the people around us who need help or desire guidance.
      2. Selective is focusing on one thing like when we read a verse or two in the Bible and spend a great deal of time thinking about its meaning.
      3. There is a right time for each.

Conclusion

Signal the End: I hope these Buddhist ideas have resonated with you.

Summary: We've examined the Four Noble Truths, the existence and origin of suffering, the cessation of creating suffering, and the eight practices that are a way to end suffering.

Final Appeal: I hope (like the thief who became a disciple of the master) that these Four Noble Truths will enlighten our lives.

Bibliography

Hanh, Thich Nhat (1998). *The heart of the Buddha's teaching.* New York, NY: Broadway Books.

Reps, Paul (1961). *Zen flesh, zen bones.* New York, NY: Doubleday Anchor Books.

Informative Speech Assignment

Rationale

This speech gives you the opportunity to put into practice and demonstrate what you have learned about selecting and researching a topic, organizing a speech, preparing an outline, delivering a speech extemporaneously, adapting to an audience, and using visual aids.

Description

1. You are to deliver a five- to seven-minute informative speech. See Chapter 13.
2. You are to prepare both a complete preparation outline and a presentation outline. See Chapter 11.
3. You are to identify which of Zarefsky's seven general purposes you are using. See Chapter 6.
4. You are to develop an appropriate specific purpose. See Chapter 6.
5. You are to craft a creative and compelling attention getter. See Chapter 10.
6. You are to build a complete introduction and conclusion. See Chapter 10.
7. You are to construct an organized body for the speech. See Chapter 9.
8. You are to use appropriate supporting materials. See Chapter 7.
9. You are to use the summary/preview format for transitions. See Chapter 10.
10. You are to design useful visual aids. See Chapter 15.
11. You are to use an extemporaneous style of delivery that is animated and enthusiastic. See Chapter 3.

Considerations

1. Was the topic appropriate for the occasion and audience?
2. Was the speech within the assigned time limit?
3. Was the introduction complete and interesting?
4. Was the speech easy to follow and remember?
5. Were the supporting materials relevant to the main points?
6. Were the supporting materials salient and adapted to the audience?
7. Did the visual aids help to clarify concepts? Did the visual aids add interest to the speech?
8. Was the delivery extemporaneous?
9. Did the speaker use a compelling style of delivery?
10. Did the speaker prepare an appropriate preparation outline?

Creating an Argument Assignment

Rationale

This assignment gives you the opportunity to practice constructing an argument by using appropriate evidence and reasoning to support that argument. This is a written assignment, but your instructor may ask you to deliver the assignment as a speech.

Description

1. Write a simple declarative sentence that represents a main claim (main point) in a persuasive speech. Use one of the main points that will be used in your persuasive speech.
2. State three pieces of evidence (supporting material) that directly support that claim.
3. Identify the type of evidence for each of the three pieces of evidence.
4. Identify the type of reasoning/inference that links the evidence to the claim.
5. Provide a complete citation using APA.

Considerations

1. Is the claim stated as a complete, simple sentence?
2. Do the three pieces of evidence directly support the claim?
3. Are the three pieces of evidence identified correctly?
4. Is the type of reasoning/inference identified correctly?
5. Are the three pieces of evidence correctly cited?

Sample Creating an Argument

Claim: Conserving energy will save you money. **Factual Claim**

Support 1: By turning off your computer instead of leaving it in sleep mode when you leave the office, you can save 40 watts of electricity a day. That adds up to 4 cents a day, or $14 per year, at the 2005 average cost of 9.45 cents per KWh.

Statistic: Gown, Michael. "8 ways to go green." *Macworld* 24.6 (June 2007), 66–68.

Reasoning by Cause: Turning off the computer (the cause) will save money.

Support 2: Laptop computers draw only 15 to 25 watts during regular use, as compared to 150 watts used by a conventional desktop computer and monitor.

Example: Howard, Brian Clark. "7 ways to save energy." *The Daily Green.* 2008.

Reasoning by Example. Comparing the examples of laptop and desktop computers prove that using laptops will save money.

Support 3: You can improve your gas mileage about 15 percent by driving at 55 mph rather than 65 mph.

Document: U.S. ENVIRONMENTAL PROTECTION AGENCY OFFICE OF MOBILE SOURCES. *Tips to Save Gas and Improve Mileage.* 2008.

Reasoning by Cause: Gas mileage will improve by reducing speed and therefore save money by using less gas to go further.

Persuasive Speech Assignment

Rationale

This assignment gives you the opportunity to put into practice and demonstrate your ability to prepare and deliver a compelling persuasive speech.

Description

1. You are to deliver a five- to seven-minute speech. See Chapter 14.
2. You are to prepare both a complete preparation outline and a presentation outline. See Chapter 11.
3. You are to identify which of Zarefsky's seven general purposes you are using. See Chapter 6.
4. You are to develop an appropriate specific purpose. See Chapter 6.
5. You are to craft a creative and compelling attention getter. See Chapter 10.
6. You are to build a complete introduction and conclusion. See Chapter 10.
7. You are to construct an organized body for the speech. See Chapters 9 and 14.
8. You are to construct compelling arguments using sound reasoning and credible evidence. See Chapters 7 and 8.
9. You are to use the summary/preview format for transitions. See Chapter 10.
10. You are to design useful visual aids. See Chapter 15.
11. You are to use an extemporaneous style of delivery that is animated and enthusiastic. See Chapter 3.
12. You are to use persuasive and memorable language. See Chapter 12.

Considerations

1. Was the topic appropriate for the occasion and audience?
2. Was the speech within the assigned time limit?
3. Was the introduction complete and interesting?
4. Was the speech easy to follow and remember?
5. Was the evidence credible?
6. Were the arguments and reasoning compelling?
7. Were the supporting materials salient and adapted to the audience?
8. Did the visual aids help to clarify concepts? Did the visual aids add interest to the speech?
9. Was the delivery extemporaneous?
10. Did the speaker use memorable language and a compelling style of delivery?
11. Did the speaker prepare an appropriate preparation outline?

Ceremonial Speaking Assignment

Rationale

Depending on your career, the most common request for you to present a speech is for a ceremonial occasion. This assignment allows you to practice your ability to connect with an audience through appropriate language and decorum for the occasion.

Description

1. You will prepare and deliver a three- to five-minute ceremonial speech. See Chapter 15.
2. You will choose one of the following types of ceremonial presentations with your instructor's agreement. See Chapter 15.
   a. Introduce a speaker
   b. Present an award
   c. Holiday speech of tribute
   d. A eulogy
   e. A toast
   f. A roast
   g. Pep talk
   h. Commencement address
3. You will exhibit the proper decorum.
4. You will gain the audience's attention.
5. You will create resonance for the audience.
6. You will use a coherent structure and development.
7. You will provide substance through supporting material for the audience.
8. You will deliver the speech with sincerity and conviction.
9. You will conclude memorably.

Considerations

1. Did the speech achieve its objective according to the type of occasion?
2. Was it memorable?
3. Was it delivered sincerely and convincingly?
4. Did the speaker use compelling language?
5. Was it easy to follow? Did it use a coherent structure?
6. Did the speech resonate with the audience? Did it establish common ground with the audience? Did it invoke common values? Did it articulate unexpressed emotion?
7. Did the speech use supporting material that was substantiative?
8. Did the speech use vivid descriptions, details, and/or examples?
9. Did the speech exhibit the proper decorum for the occasion?

Impromptu Speech Assignment

(20 points)

Rationale

If time permits, your instructor may assign this type of speech. This is the most common form of public speaking. You experience it every class period when you answer a question or make a comment during discussion. You also will have many opportunities to voice your opinions and concerns at public meetings, professional meetings, and other types of group meetings. This assignment is designed to give you the opportunity to practice speaking articulately and well in those circumstances.

Descriptions

1. Your instructor will give you a topic in the form of a word or quotation and you will have five minutes to prepare a five-minute speech.
2. You are to prepare an introduction with an attention getter, thesis, and preview.
3. You are to develop the thesis with main points.
4. You are to clarify the main points with supporting material.
5. You are to use transitions between the main points.
6. You are to prepare a conclusion with a summary and an impact statement.

Considerations

1. Did the speech capture the audience's attention?
2. Is the speech easy to follow?
3. Is the thesis clear?
4. Did the main points develop the thesis as stated?
5. Were the supporting materials relevant and salient?
6. Was the conclusion effective?
7. Was the delivery animated and enthusiastic?

Grading and Evaluation Sheets

This section contains the tear-out sheets that you will be giving to your instructor and fellow classmates. Please make sure to bring your handbook to every class.

Speech of Introduction Audience Reaction Sheet

Speaker: ____

The best part of this speech was . . .

The things that could be improved were . . .

Speech of Introduction Audience Reaction Sheet

Speaker: ____

The best part of this speech was . . .

The things that could be improved were . . .

Speech of Introduction Audience Reaction Sheet

Speaker: ____

The best part of this speech was . . .

The things that could be improved were . . .

Speech of Introduction Audience Reaction Sheet

Speaker: ____

The best part of this speech was . . .

The things that could be improved were . . .

Speech of Introduction Audience Reaction Sheet

Speaker: ____

The best part of this speech was . . .

The things that could be improved were . . .

Speech of Introduction Audience Reaction Sheet

Speaker: ____

The best part of this speech was . . .

The things that could be improved were . . .

Supporting a Main Point Instructor Critique

Speaker: ____________________

Comments:

Introduction:

Attention getter

Thesis

Disposition to speaker and topic

Preview

Body:

Structure

Supporting material

Transition/signposts

Conclusion:

Summary

Impact statement

Delivery:

Extemporaneous

Eye contact

Expressiveness/animation

Rate

Gesture/movement

Articulation

Enunciation

Pronunciation

Visual Aids:

Supporting a Main Point Audience Reaction Sheet

Speaker: ______________________________

Was the main point clear? Why? Why not?

Did the supporting material clarify or develop the main point as stated? Why? Why not?

The best part of this speech was . . .

Things that need improvement are . . .

Supporting a Main Point Audience Reaction Sheet

Speaker: ______________________________

Was the main point clear? Why? Why not?

Did the supporting material clarify or develop the main point as stated? Why? Why not?

The best part of this speech was . . .

Things that need improvement are . . .

Supporting a Main Point Audience Reaction Sheet

Speaker: ____

Was the main point clear? Why? Why not?

Did the supporting material clarify or develop the main point as stated? Why? Why not?

The best part of this speech was . . .

Things that need improvement are . . .

Supporting a Main Point Audience Reaction Sheet

Speaker: ____

Was the main point clear? Why? Why not?

Did the supporting material clarify or develop the main point as stated? Why? Why not?

The best part of this speech was . . .

Things that need improvement are . . .

Supporting a Main Point Audience Reaction Sheet

Speaker: ____

Was the main point clear?   Why?   Why not?

Did the supporting material clarify or develop the main point as stated?   Why?   Why not?

The best part of this speech was . . .

Things that need improvement are . . .

Supporting a Main Point Audience Reaction Sheet

Speaker: ____

Was the main point clear?   Why?   Why not?

Did the supporting material clarify or develop the main point as stated?   Why?   Why not?

The best part of this speech was . . .

Things that need improvement are . . .

Informative Speech Audience Evaluation Sheet

Speaker: ______________________________

Audience Member: ______________________________

I found the topic interesting. Yes No

Was the attention getter creative? Yes No
Was the thesis statement clearly stated? Yes No
The thesis statement was . . .

Was there a preview of the main points? Yes No
The main points were . . .

Did the supporting material clarify and develop the main points? Yes No
Did the speaker orally footnote the supporting material? Yes No

Transitions made the speech easy to follow. Yes No

Did the speaker signal the conclusion? Yes No
Did the speaker summarize the main points? Yes No
The impact statement was . . .

The visual aids were interesting. Yes No
The visual aids were used. Yes No
I felt I learned something I needed to know or was interested in knowing. Yes No

What were the best things about the speaker's delivery of the speech?

What aspects of the speaker's delivery need some improvement?

Overall impression of the speech: poor average good excellent

Informative Speech Audience Evaluation Sheet

Speaker: ____

Audience Member: ____

I found the topic interesting. Yes No

Was the attention getter creative? Yes No
Was the thesis statement clearly stated? Yes No
The thesis statement was . . .

Was there a preview of the main points? Yes No
he main points were . . .

he supporting material clarify and develop the main points? Yes No
e speaker orally footnote the supporting material? Yes No

ons made the speech easy to follow. Yes No

peaker signal the conclusion? Yes No
peaker summarize the main points? Yes No
ct statement was . . .

The visual aids were interesting. Yes No
The visual aids were used. Yes No
I felt I learned something I needed to know or was interested in knowing. Yes No

What were the best things about the speaker's delivery of the speech?

What aspects of the speaker's delivery need some improvement?

Overall impression of the speech: poor average good excellent

Informative Speech Audience Evaluation Sheet

Speaker: ____

Audience Member: ______________________________________

I found the topic interesting. Yes No

Was the attention getter creative? Yes No
Was the thesis statement clearly stated? Yes No
The thesis statement was . . .

Was there a preview of the main points? Yes No
The main points were . . .

Did the supporting material clarify and develop the main points? Yes No
Did the speaker orally footnote the supporting material? Yes No

Transitions made the speech easy to follow. Yes No

Did the speaker signal the conclusion? Yes No
Did the speaker summarize the main points? Yes No
The impact statement was . . .

The visual aids were interesting. Yes No
The visual aids were used. Yes No
I felt I learned something I needed to know or was interested in knowing. Yes No

What were the best things about the speaker's delivery of the speech?

What aspects of the speaker's delivery need some improvement?

Overall impression of the speech: poor average good excellent

Informative Speech Audience Evaluation Sheet

Speaker: ____________________

Audience Member: ____________________

I found the topic interesting. Yes No

Was the attention getter creative? Yes No
Was the thesis statement clearly stated? Yes No
The thesis statement was . . .

Was there a preview of the main points? Yes No
The main points were . . .

Did the supporting material clarify and develop the main points? Yes No
Did the speaker orally footnote the supporting material? Yes No

Transitions made the speech easy to follow. Yes No

Did the speaker signal the conclusion? Yes No
Did the speaker summarize the main points? Yes No
The impact statement was . . .

The visual aids were interesting. Yes No
The visual aids were used. Yes No
I felt I learned something I needed to know or was interested in knowing. Yes No

What were the best things about the speaker's delivery of the speech?

What aspects of the speaker's delivery need some improvement?

Overall impression of the speech: poor average good excellent

Informative Speech Audience Evaluation Sheet

Speaker: ______________________________

Audience Member: ______________________________

I found the topic interesting. Yes No

Was the attention getter creative? Yes No
Was the thesis statement clearly stated? Yes No
The thesis statement was . . .

Was there a preview of the main points? Yes No
The main points were . . .

Did the supporting material clarify and develop the main points? Yes No
Did the speaker orally footnote the supporting material? Yes No

Transitions made the speech easy to follow. Yes No

Did the speaker signal the conclusion? Yes No
Did the speaker summarize the main points? Yes No
The impact statement was . . .

The visual aids were interesting. Yes No
The visual aids were used. Yes No
I felt I learned something I needed to know or was interested in knowing. Yes No

What were the best things about the speaker's delivery of the speech?

What aspects of the speaker's delivery need some improvement?

Overall impression of the speech: poor average good excellent

Creating an Argument Audience Reaction Sheet

Speaker: ____

Was the claim clear? Why? Why not?

Did the evidence support the claim as stated? Why? Why not?

The best part of this speech was . . .

Things that need improvement are . . .

Creating an Argument Audience Reaction Sheet

Speaker: ____

Was the claim clear? Why? Why not?

Did the evidence support the claim as stated? Why? Why not?

The best part of this speech was . . .

Things that need improvement are . . .

Creating an Argument Audience Reaction Sheet

Speaker: ______________________________

Was the claim clear? Why? Why not?

Did the evidence support the claim as stated? Why? Why not?

The best part of this speech was . . .

Things that need improvement are . . .

Creating an Argument Audience Reaction Sheet

Speaker: ______________________________

Was the claim clear? Why? Why not?

Did the evidence support the claim as stated? Why? Why not?

The best part of this speech was . . .

Things that need improvement are . . .

Creating an Argument Audience Reaction Sheet

Speaker: ____

Was the claim clear? Why? Why not?

Did the evidence support the claim as stated? Why? Why not?

The best part of this speech was . . .

Things that need improvement are . . .

Creating an Argument Audience Reaction Sheet

Speaker: ____

Was the claim clear? Why? Why not?

Did the evidence support the claim as stated? Why? Why not?

The best part of this speech was . . .

Things that need improvement are . . .

Creating an Argument Instructor Critique

Speaker: ______________________________

Comments:

Introduction:

Attention getter

Claim

Disposition to speaker and topic

Preview

Body:

Structure

Evidence and reasoning

Transition/signposts

Conclusion:

Summary

Impact statement

Delivery:

Extemporaneous

Eye contact

Expressiveness/animation

Rate

Gesture/movement

Articulation

Enunciation

Pronunciation

Visual Aids:

Persuasive Speech Audience Evaluation Sheet

Speaker: ____

Audience Member: ______________________________________

I found the topic compelling. Yes No

Was the attention getter creative? Yes No
Was the thesis clearly stated? Yes No
The thesis statement was . . .

Was there a preview of the main points/claims? Yes No
The main points/claims were . . .

Did the evidence support the main points/claims? Yes No
Did the speaker orally footnote the evidence? Yes No

Transitions made the speech easy to follow. Yes No
Did the speaker use an appropriate organizational pattern? Yes No
The organizational pattern was . . .

Did the speaker signal the conclusion? Yes No
Did the speaker summarize the main points/claims? Yes No
The impact statement was . . .

I was convinced that the thesis was true. Yes No Maybe
My beliefs, attitudes, values, or behavior will be changed because of this speech. Yes No Maybe

What were the best things about the speaker's delivery of the speech?

What aspects of the speaker's delivery need some improvement?

Persuasive Speech Audience Evaluation Sheet

Speaker: ____

Audience Member: ______________________________________

I found the topic compelling. Yes No

Was the attention getter creative? Yes No
Was the thesis clearly stated? Yes No
The thesis statement was . . .

Was there a preview of the main points/claims? Yes No
The main points/claims were . . .

Did the evidence support the main points/claims? Yes No
Did the speaker orally footnote the evidence? Yes No

Transitions made the speech easy to follow. Yes No
Did the speaker use an appropriate organizational pattern? Yes No
The organizational pattern was . . .

Did the speaker signal the conclusion? Yes No
Did the speaker summarize the main points/claims? Yes No
The impact statement was . . .

I was convinced that the thesis was true. Yes No Maybe
My beliefs, attitudes, values, or behavior will be changed because of this speech. Yes No Maybe

What were the best things about the speaker's delivery of the speech?

What aspects of the speaker's delivery need some improvement?

Persuasive Speech Audience Evaluation Sheet

Speaker: ____

Audience Member: ____

I found the topic compelling. Yes No

Was the attention getter creative? Yes No
Was the thesis clearly stated? Yes No
The thesis statement was . . .

Was there a preview of the main points/claims? Yes No
The main points/claims were . . .

Did the evidence support the main points/claims? Yes No
Did the speaker orally footnote the evidence? Yes No

Transitions made the speech easy to follow. Yes No
Did the speaker use an appropriate organizational pattern? Yes No
The organizational pattern was . . .

Did the speaker signal the conclusion? Yes No
Did the speaker summarize the main points/claims? Yes No
The impact statement was . . .

I was convinced that the thesis was true. Yes No Maybe
My beliefs, attitudes, values, or behavior will be changed because of this speech. Yes No Maybe

What were the best things about the speaker's delivery of the speech?

What aspects of the speaker's delivery need some improvement?

Persuasive Speech Audience Evaluation Sheet

Speaker: ____

Audience Member: ______________________________________

I found the topic compelling. Yes No

Was the attention getter creative? Yes No
Was the thesis clearly stated? Yes No
The thesis statement was . . .

Was there a preview of the main points/claims? Yes No
The main points/claims were . . .

Did the evidence support the main points/claims? Yes No
Did the speaker orally footnote the evidence? Yes No

Transitions made the speech easy to follow. Yes No
Did the speaker use an appropriate organizational pattern? Yes No
The organizational pattern was . . .

Did the speaker signal the conclusion? Yes No
Did the speaker summarize the main points/claims? Yes No
The impact statement was . . .

I was convinced that the thesis was true. Yes No Maybe
My beliefs, attitudes, values, or behavior will be changed because of this speech. Yes No Maybe

What were the best things about the speaker's delivery of the speech?

What aspects of the speaker's delivery need some improvement?

Persuasive Speech Audience Evaluation Sheet

Speaker: ______________________________

Audience Member: ______________________________

I found the topic compelling. Yes No

Was the attention getter creative? Yes No
Was the thesis clearly stated? Yes No
The thesis statement was . . .

Was there a preview of the main points/claims? Yes No
The main points/claims were . . .

Did the evidence support the main points/claims? Yes No
Did the speaker orally footnote the evidence? Yes No

Transitions made the speech easy to follow. Yes No
Did the speaker use an appropriate organizational pattern? Yes No
The organizational pattern was . . .

Did the speaker signal the conclusion? Yes No
Did the speaker summarize the main points/claims? Yes No
The impact statement was . . .

I was convinced that the thesis was true. Yes No Maybe
My beliefs, attitudes, values, or behavior will be changed because of this speech. Yes No Maybe

What were the best things about the speaker's delivery of the speech?

What aspects of the speaker's delivery need some improvement?

Persuasive Speech Audience Evaluation Sheet

Speaker: ______________________________

Audience Member: ______________________________

I found the topic compelling. Yes No

Was the attention getter creative? Yes No
Was the thesis clearly stated? Yes No
The thesis statement was . . .

Was there a preview of the main points/claims? Yes No
The main points/claims were . . .

Did the evidence support the main points/claims? Yes No
Did the speaker orally footnote the evidence? Yes No

Transitions made the speech easy to follow. Yes No
Did the speaker use an appropriate organizational pattern? Yes No
The organizational pattern was . . .

Did the speaker signal the conclusion? Yes No
Did the speaker summarize the main points/claims? Yes No
The impact statement was . . .

I was convinced that the thesis was true. Yes No Maybe
My beliefs, attitudes, values, or behavior will be changed because of this speech. Yes No Maybe

What were the best things about the speaker's delivery of the speech?

What aspects of the speaker's delivery need some improvement?

Ceremonial Speech Grading Sheet
(50 points)

Speaker: ______________________________

Ceremonial Occasion: ______________________________

Rating Scale: 5 = excellent; 4 = very good; 3 = satisfactory; 2 = unsatisfactory;
1 = poor; 0 = nonexistent

Comments:

_______ Gains attention and interest

_______ Establishes common ground

_______ Resonates with audience

_______ Articulates unexpressed emotion

_______ Appropriate structure

_______ Fulfills goals

_______ Provides substance

_______ Uses vivid descriptions, details, and examples

_______ Exhibits appropriate decorum

_______ Demonstrates sincerity and conviction

Overall impression:

Impromptu Speech Grading Sheet

(20 points)

Speaker: ______________________________ Speaking Time: __________

Rating Scale: 4 = excellent; 3 = very good; 2 = average; 1 = poor; 0 = nonexistent

Comments:

_______ Complete introduction

_______ Easily followed

_______ Relevant supporting material

_______ Effective conclusion

_______ Delivery

Overall impression:

Advice and Activities

This section contains a few activities to help you practice some concepts you will be learning in the class and a little advice about selecting topics.

Scrambled Outline Exercise

Below you will find a series of sentences for a persuasive outline, including a specific purpose statement, introduction, body, transition statements, and conclusion. Arrange the numbered sentences in a logical manner using the outline format on the following page.

1. Caffeine dangers can be reduced.
2. Caffeine can have a potentially toxic effect.
3. Let's look at the dangers of caffeine and then determine how to best protect ourselves.
4. Evidence clearly indicates that caffeine is a drug that can endanger our health.
5. Caffeine does a lot more than perk you up.
6. Social rules encourage the consumption of caffeine.
7. Caffeine is an addictive drug.
8. Public education is needed.
9. Caffeine is a socially accepted but potentially dangerous drug.
10. Because caffeine is so dangerously pervasive, steps need to be taken to lessen its potential harm.
11. I'm useless until I have my morning coffee.
12. Caffeine is a drug that acts on the central nervous system.
13. Caffeine is the most widely consumed, mind-affecting substance in the world.
14. A "safe level" of caffeine is 250 milligrams a day.
15. The best bet is to eat a healthy breakfast and skip the coffee.
16. Caffeine may be related to physical problems.
17. Obviously, caffeine adversely affects us, but we still consume it.
18. Individuals must make a conscious effort to monitor their caffeine intake.
19. Conservative estimates show that at least 10 percent of adults consume 1,000 milligrams a day.
20. Caffeine is in many products, not just coffee.
21. I want my audience to reduce their consumption of caffeine.

Scrambled Outline Answer Sheet

Purpose Statement:

Introduction:

A.
B.
C.

Body:

I.
  A.
  B.
  C.

Transition:

II.
  A.
  B.
  C.
    1.
    2.

Transition:

III.
  A.
  B.

Conclusion:

A.
B.

Selecting a Topic

Most students find selecting a topic one of the most difficult aspects of this course. It may be useful to think of topic selection for an informative speech as an opportunity to learn something new and interesting, or as an opportunity to share something you know with your fellow classmates. Your topic should be interesting to you, interesting to your audience, and appropriate to the assignment.

One way is to think in general categories and then list things that come to your mind. General categories for an informative speech might include: **people, places, events, recreation activities, concepts, processes,** or **events**. The person or people you research should have had an effect on or do affect the lives of others. They can be writers, artists, scientists, or politicians, etc., from the past or the present. It is always interesting to know more about people who influence others and why. Vividly describing interesting places that you've visited or would like to visit, or examining historical or current events that have had or have an impact on us can be exciting. There are a lot of ideas and concepts out there that influence how we live, and many of us would like to know how something works or how to do something.

Always remember that you will need to connect the topic to the audience. You will need to answer their question, "Why do I need to know this?" and "Why should I listen to this?" Sometimes the best topics tell your audience things they didn't know about common things, and sometimes the best topic is one that tells them about something new. For example, we all are familiar with quilts, but a speech about quilt patterns that sent signals to escaping slaves on the Underground Railroad is interesting. One of the most useful student speeches I listened to was in the early 1990s about identity theft. This was long before the problem was common knowledge. While you're watching, reading, or listening, pay particular attention to things that spark your curiosity. You and your audience are very similar in many ways, and the things that interest you are probably the same things that will interest them.

General categories for a persuasive speech might include: **local, national, international,** or **personal issues**. The topic should be relatively controversial, and you should be taking a stance your audience does not embrace. Remember, a persuasive speech attempts to effect a change of belief, attitude, values, or behavior in your audience. In other words, don't preach to the choir. One of the best ways to choose a persuasive topic is to consider things that have annoyed or bothered you. If you've ever said to yourself, "Somebody oughta do something!" then that might make a good persuasive topic. Again, pay attention to the things you are watching, reading, or listening to, and if something sparks your concern or outrages you, it might make a good topic for persuasion.

The brainstorming activity on the following page should help you choose a unique and interesting topic. Try to stay away from overused classroom topics unless you can bring something new to the audience. Your instructor may have a list of these topics for you.

Selecting a Topic for Informative Speaking

Brainstorming Activity

As quickly as you can (without censoring), make a list under each category.

Recreation	Concepts	Places	Objects	People	Processes	Events
Music	Dreams	Spain	Toilets	Reagan	Making beer	Woodstock

Check your lists and determine which would be most interesting to you and your audience as well as which would be best suited for an informative speech. Then, make a spidergram to help you begin to narrow down the topic. If needed, make another spidergram to help you decide how to approach the topic.

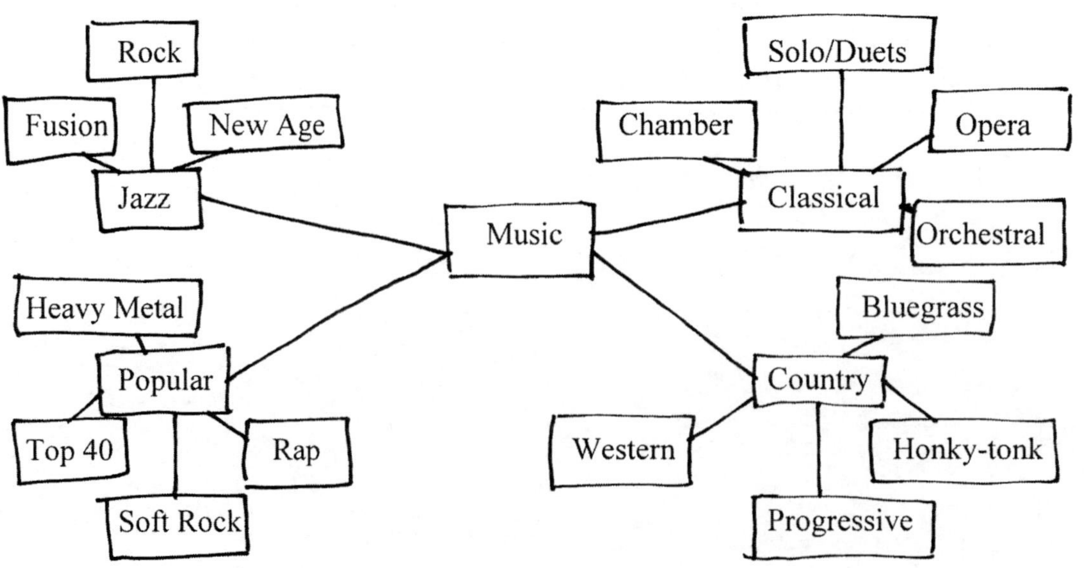

Selecting a Topic for a Persuasive Speech

Brainstorming Activity

As quickly as you can (without censoring), make a list under each category or make up your own general categories. Keep in mind that you are thinking about something that is controversial or needs to be changed.

Environment	Sports	Education	Health	National	International	Entertainment
Gulf oil spill	Drug testing	No Child Left Behind	Flu shots	Flat tax	Terrorism	Reality TV

Check your lists and determine which would be most interesting to you and your audience as well as which would be best suited for a persuasive speech. Then, make a spidergram to help you begin to narrow down the topic and/or the issues surrounding that topic.

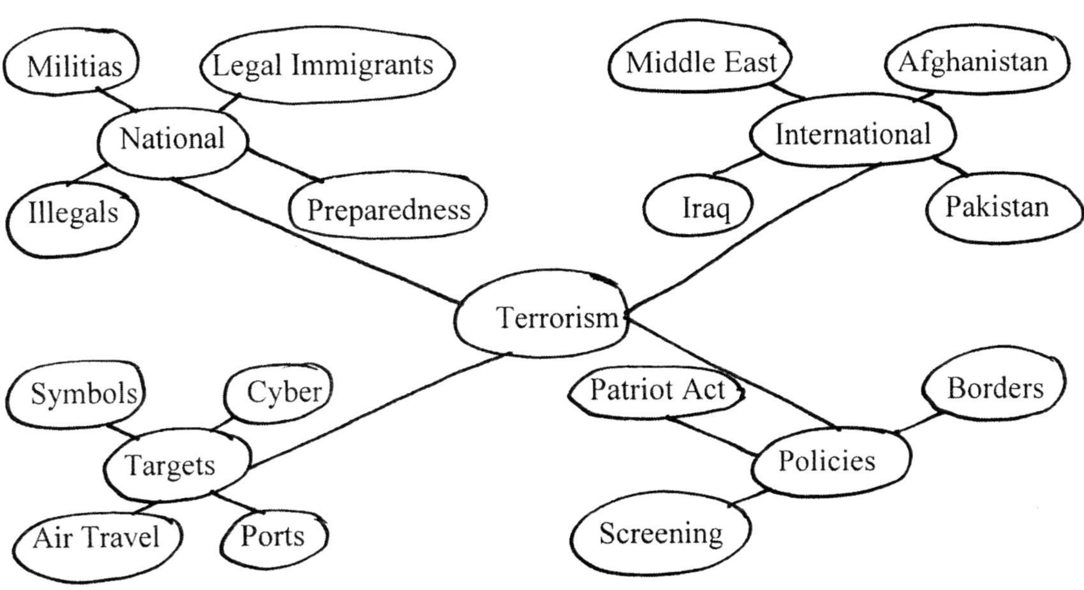

Identify the Type of Claim

Instructions: Read the following statements and indicate whether it is a factual claim, a value claim, or a policy claim.

Example: Sex education programs in high schools decrease the amount of teen pregnancies. *Fact Claim*

An abstinence-only approach to sex education is the most moral way to teach sex education. *Value Claim*

All high schools in the United States should mandate that students complete a unit on sexual education. *Policy Claim*

1. Capitalism is an unjust economic system.
2. Marshall University should allow their students to create their own major.
3. The attack on Pearl Harbor forced the United States to be involved in World War II.
4. Capital punishment deters crime.
5. Every American should be made to take a flu shot.
6. Chicago is the greatest city in America.
7. The crime rate in Huntington, WV will decrease in the next five years.
8. The consumption of meat by humans is unethical.
9. On average, students who attend graduate school make more money than those who do not.
10. Drinking milk on a daily basis is good for your bones.
11. It is immoral to not participate in recycling programs.
12. Turkey hunting season ought to be limited to the week during Thanksgiving.
13. Watching TV is a waste of time.
14. Chocolate is the best flavor of ice cream.
15. The United States federal government should pass a law limiting Internet neutrality.
16. National security is always more important than personal privacy in times of war.
17. West Virginia should pass a law banning mountaintop removal for the purpose of mining coal.
18. *Seinfeld* was a much better show than *Cheers*.
19. The NCAA should do away with the Bowl Championship Series.
20. Parents of newborns ought to have more time off from work.

Impromptu Topics

Sell the following item:

Cheerios
BlackBerry
Bananas
Watermelons
Converse sneakers
Timex watch
iPod
Netflix
A VCR
Circular saw
A hammer
Grass seed
A rake
BP gasoline
A bicycle
Bic pens
Dixon pencils
Crayola crayons

Which is better?

Jelly or peanut butter
Soccer or football
Pens or pencils
Apples or oranges
HP or Dell
Reality or fantasy
E-mail or snail mail
Cats or dogs
Cars or motorcycles
Mountains or beaches
Morning, afternoon, or night
North or south
East coast or West coast
Books, movies, or TV
Las Vegas or Atlantic City
Rivers or lakes
Love or friendship
Brothers or sisters

Vividly describe the following item:

Broccoli
Green beans
Cell phones
Snow
The ocean
Satin sheets
FOX cable news
MSNBC cable news
Tulips
Roses
Rain
Briefcases
Hip Hop music
Jazz
Concerts
Rock & roll
College classes
Marshall University
Huntington
Ohio River

Scrambled Outline Answer Key

Purpose Statement: I want my audience to reduce their consumption of caffeine.

Introduction

A. I'm useless until I have my morning coffee.
B. Caffeine is the most widely consumed, mind-affecting substance in the world.
C. Let's look at the dangers of caffeine and then determine how to best protect ourselves from its effect.

Body

I. Caffeine does a lot more than perk you up.
    A. Caffeine is a drug that acts on the central nervous system.
    B. Caffeine is an addictive drug.
    C. Caffeine may be related to physical problems.

Transition: Obviously, caffeine adversely affects us, but we still consume it.

II. Caffeine is a socially accepted but potentially dangerous drug.
    A. Social rules encourage the consumption of caffeine.
    B. Caffeine is in many products, not just coffee.
    C. Caffeine can have a potentially toxic effect.
        1. A "safe level" of caffeine is 250 milligrams a day.
        2. Conservative estimates show that at least 10 percent of adults consume 1,000 milligrams a day.

Transition: Because caffeine is so dangerously pervasive, steps need to be taken to lessen its potential harm.

III. Caffeine dangers can be reduced.
    A. Public education is needed.
    B. Individuals must make a conscious effort to monitor their caffeine intake.

Conclusion

A. Evidence clearly indicates that caffeine is a drug that can endanger our health.
B. The best bet is to eat a healthy breakfast and skip the coffee.

Dear CMM Basic Course Student:

As part of our ongoing effort to improve the quality of our curriculum, we are engaged in research to identify the basic speaking skill level of students who have completed our oral communication courses. In order to perform this assessment, we need a sample of students persuasive speeches for review. Your speech may be randomly selected, so I am asking you to agree to participate in our annual review.

Your recorded speech, and those of the other students in the sample, would be reviewed over the summer by the Director of the Basic Course and two other instructors. You will not be identified by name or student number. We would simply be viewing the sample speeches to determine the level of basic communication skills evident in our sample so that we can determine how successful we have been in teaching basic principles of organizing, supporting, and presenting ideas. ***This review will not affect your grade in the course in any way.***

You have the right to refuse to participate in this assessment procedure. Our assessment of the course is not a part of any student's grade. However, I am asking you to help us by contributing your speech.

I hope that you will allow us to use your speech in our sample this year. You may signify your permission by signing the form below.

Thank you for your cooperation. Your assistance is of considerable value to our program's efforts to maintain a high quality of instruction in our basic courses.

Respectfully,

Kristine L. Greenwood, PhD

Director of the Basic Course in Oral Communication
Department of Communication Studies
Marshall University

I grant the Director of the Basic Course in Oral Communication permission to use my videotaped speech in the annual assessment of Marshall University's oral communication requirement.

Student Signature ____________________________ ***Date*** ______________________

Course/Section Number ________________